AF338272

Advance Praise for *Learning to Jump*

"*Learning to Jump* is a book full of character, color, and intimacy. These are unhurried, intricately observed poems that fall onto the page like leaves, cherished things slowly brought back into the light. Sean McDowell is a poet who illuminates the bonds that lightly (so lightly we hardly notice) hold us together and keep us from falling apart. Here we wander with a wanderer, a scholar who has left his library, and we travel far, from Seattle's Pacific Northwest to rain-soaked Connemara in the west of Ireland, to explore what might be gained or lost along the way."
—Tony Curtis, author of *This Flight Tonight*

"We have long celebrated Sean McDowell's many achievements as critic, teacher, editor, and executive director of the John Donne Society. This book demonstrates his impressive poetic gifts. He has an ear and a mind and a heart for sound effects, for precise and often surprising words, and for startlingly original images. Many poems explore details of the natural, everyday world, where, in these moving lyrics, the secular and spiritual interact and intersect."
—Heather Dubrow, John D. Boyd, SJ, Chair in Poetic Imagination, Fordham University

"*Learning How to Jump* transports the reader to 'a place / that is no place and every place / at the heart of heartfelt melody.' At the heart of the poet's heartfelt melodics, you'll find several achingly beautiful love poems. This is a wonderful book with fresh poems you will return to again

and again with deepening pleasure. There's a daring newness, too, in how Sean McDowell uses plain, direct speech. I applaud the new possibilities he brings to our time."
—Greg Miller, professor emeritus of English, Millsaps College

"Under his poet's gaze, the small and common things of the world ascend into Sean McDowell's nearly reverent attention to be simultaneously affirmed as needful in themselves and expanded into resonances beyond themselves. As McDowell urges his reader, over and again in a variety of ways, to 'Look closely,' so he enlists us in the extraordinary work of being enthralled by the ordinary."
—Kimberly Johnson, author of *Fatal*

"There is a peculiar state we enter when we've read a good poem, a sort of 'post-poem' reverie, eyes unfocused, turned inward, a letting go of barriers, allowing whatever might come to go ahead and change our lives. Reading McDowell, I find myself in this welcome condition over and over. He combines the discipline and patience of an internationally acclaimed scholar with a sensibility that recognizes the difference between poems that can be written and, like these, ones that should be. I love this book."
—Samuel Green, author of *Disturbing the Light*

Learning to Jump

Also by Sean McDowell:

*Metaphysical Shadows: The Persistence of Donne, Herbert,
Vaughan, and Marvell in Contemporary Poetry*

O

LEARNING TO JUMP

Poems by

Sean McDowell

O

RESOURCE *Publications* · Eugene, Oregon

Resource Publications
A Division of Wipf and Stock Publishers
199 W. 8th Ave., Suite 3
Eugene, OR 97401

www.wipfandstock.com

Library of Congress Cataloging-in-Publication Data is available.

Paperback ISBN: 978-1-6667-8457-2
Hardcover ISBN: 978-1-6667-8458-9
eBook ISBN: 978-1-6667-8459-6

For Andrea, Tessa, Kieran, and Jensen

Acknowledgements

Several poems in this collection first appeared, in earlier and sometimes different forms, in the following publications: *Poetry Ireland Review* and *The Madrona Project* ("Chicken Soup"); *The Lyric* ("Connemara Village"); *Cirque: A Literary Journal of the North Pacific Rim* ("Between Two Rivers in Galway"); *Clover, a literary rag* ("Ice and Stone," "Stone Trough on Inis Mór," and "Leaf"); *Fragments* ("Heliotropism"); *Vine Leaves Literary Journal* and *The Best of Vine Leaves 2014* ("Tooth"); *Scintilla* ("Wind at Dún Aonghasa," "Photogram," "Driftwood," and "Mustard Jug"); and *The High Window* ("Egg Tempera," "Homemade Wine on the 4th of July," "My Aunt, Sketching," "Shelf Building," "Birthday Wish," "Clock," "Perfume Bottles," "Arts of the Book," "Lecture upon a Pigeon," "Keepsake," and "Rosary"). My thanks to the editors of these publications for first seeing these poems into print, and in a larger sense, for their dedication to the work.

Over the course of many years, I have benefited greatly from the conversation, inspiration, and kind words of a variety of encouragers along the way, especially the late Judith H. Anderson, Susan Jensen, Beth and Gib Rossing, George Klawitter, Raymond-Jean Frontain, Judith Scherer Herz, Achsah Guibbory, Gary Stringer, Jeanne Shami, Jonathan F. S. Post, Dayton Haskin, Maria Salenius, Kirsten Stirling, Greg Kneidel, Brent Nelson, Angela Balla, Frank Zychowicz, Darlene Poczekaj, Jeanne Zychowicz, Mike and Jill Perkins, Bill Taylor, Jim Risser, Dean Peterson, Thorne Clayton-Falls, Jason Wirth, Gabriella Gutiérrez y Muhs, Mark Pigott, Heather Dubrow, Paula Meehan, Theo Dorgan, Greg Miller, Kimberly Johnson, Anne-Marie Miller-Blaise, Tony Curtis, Mary Canavan, Edwin and Noreen Weihe, and Sam and Sally Green. Always steadfast in her support, my mother Virginia Lofendo was among the first to cheer the writing of these poems. This book is for my wife Andrea and our children Tessa, Kieran, and Jensen, who fill my days with light.

Contents

LEARNING TO JUMP

No matter then although my foot did stand
Upon the farthest earth remov'd from thee;
For nimble thought can jump both sea and land,
As soon as think the place where he would be.

William Shakespeare, "Sonnet 44"

Fiddler in the Church

She played this slow air yesterday
at her grandmother's funeral.

Long, deliberate strokes in the Galway style,
long, high notes meant for wind

over limestone in all kinds of weather,
low notes, like the knelling

of the day's last light, changeable
in the creeping way of clouds—

then   *crash!*   *clatter!*   a cell phone
dropped startles us back to ourselves.

The fiddler charms
the embarrassed silence.

Freshets of sound echo and rebound
off fourteenth-century arches.

Her air throbs and drawls and keens
and carries us to a place

that is no place and every place
at the heart of heartfelt melody.

Chicken Soup

She threw away what others most relied on:
neck bones, gizzards, bent wings, and livers,
the carcass after the choice cuts were gone.
Even thigh bones and drumsticks, which neighbors bought
fried by the bucket, never graced her pot.

And tailbones, *What good could come from a dead
bird's ass?* She rinsed and trimmed four raw breasts
of excess rubbery skin, covered them
with cold water and poured in salt measured
from her practiced palm. Her vegetables

followed with like care. After peeling away
their papery skin, she burned both
the tops and bottoms of two large onions
until they blackened on an open flame.
Then three celery stalks (leaves intact)

and three carrots she snicked into thick rounds.
Next she coaxed the crammed pot to boiling,
then set it simmering, slowly skimming
off the grit and froth of muddying fat
as offensive to the true faith of broth.

By and by the boiling meat wept bubbles
of pure gold, and golden too the essences
leached from the rest till the burgeoning soup
began darkening to a lager's hue,
its smell warming the kitchen like a presence.

Outside, past the forked oaks, beyond the plain
below her hill, the shipping cranes on Maumee Bay
looked toylike in the distance and so did
the cargo ships bound for continents
my grandmother would never travel to.

By and by onions clarified. Carrots
softened. Celery went limp. And meat
sloughed off bones. She strained every solid
and morsel from the clear broth and added
nothing but Kluski noodles, their fetal curls.

So she ladled her every ambition
into the anonymity of the shallow bowl
she offered me. And so I slurped each spoonful
in disbelief that anything this precious
could be mine for as long as it lasted.

Tooth

His front tooth, once apple solid,
now lifts like a tab on an Advent calendar.
I give him a wet washcloth to staunch the blood
and tell him to work it, not up and down
but side to side in a gentle twist.
The pain of last connection soon comes due:
he shouts in mini-labor, twists again,
and effortlessly it breaks free, smaller now,
a flattened freshwater pearl chipped at one end.
The hole in that grin, dripping blood,
all over his lower lip, looks huge,
one more of those befores and afters
reminding us we never can go back.

Wind at Dún Aonghasa

for Gib Rossing

Here in the innermost wall
it spades all the open places
and spreads across face and hands
like sunburn. Constant as water's
embrace, it softens a tour guide's
barked guttural German into
something like normal conversation.
It muffles the buzzing of horse flies
and the cries of gulls floating
like open books someone
fell asleep while reading.
It deadens the whoosh and crash
of surf below.
           And yet the longer
you listen, the more it resembles
circulation, the kind you hear when
you cover an ear with a water glass
or the flayed mouth of a conch shell.
Something larger than any of us breathes.
Here, where only shy things grow,
the wind is the voice the world
uses when neither you nor I
nor anyone else can interject.
It belongs in the gaps between
unmortared stones.

Learning to Jump

for Andrea

Beacon Hill Park: rhodies in bloom,
cherry blossoms about to snow,
thick bushes abuzz in nectar-
gathering. Scores of blue herons

nested in tall trees, their chattering
a heavy downpour, remember?
Then out again into sunlight
and farther down, the petting zoo.

A cluster of red and white barns
within a stacked log fence, the yard
softened by woodchips and also
abuzz with the wee snorts, bleats,

and clucks of piglets, lambs, ducklings,
and hopping, bounding, jostling
goats—precarious kids on the loose,
hours-old weights on stilts, jumping.

In the goathouse, crowds gathered
round the fetid stalls to watch new
Spring births. We arrived in time
to see a Nigerian dwarf doe

panting on her side in
the high-altitude of labor
against the full-body struggle
of the widening birth canal.

She screeched with each push,
the last so loud the woman beside me
clutched my arm in a death grip.
Sorry—an embarrassed smile—

that brought back memories. Your lips
were parted, your eyes shone, your right
hand casually stroked your belly.
Rustle of straw, kick, breathless strain—

the newborn slipped out
shockingly fast. It stood, slick
and tottering, while the weary
mother sighed into an afterwards.

Hand-in-hand, we ventured outside
to admire the rest—how they learned
to jump before bothering to walk
and damned if they cared where they might land.

Martini

The thick box flaps are stiff and sharp enough
to slice fingers. So I unfold them with
the same care of one who has been cut before.

Inside, sturdy dividers silo
the remaining bottles of Stolichnaya
as if they might explode on contact.

I fish out a fresh one, re-braid the flaps,
and heave the case back onto its dusty shelf.
A sharp twist breaks the perforated seal.

The cap turns easily. Vodka looks like
water through clear glass but smells like bug spray.
The ice cube tray won't give. I have to crack

its back against the edge of the counter.
Each cube pings the crystal glass like a call
to order. I measure in four ice-

crackling shots. Next, a shot of dry Vermouth
(like pineapple gone sour) and three pimentoed
olives because I know he'll ask for more

than two. The latest college game fantails
sparks of crowd noise into the living room.
He lounges, immoveable, in his fat

recliner, illegal pad well-columned
in losses and wins. I am ten years old.
I must carry the cold glass with both hands,

fix my gaze on the brim, and shuffle
with slow, sleepwalker steps to cross
the room and avoid spilling his anger.

Photogram

i.m. Larry Mohler

My uncle taught me the inverse of light,
the radiance of shadows and inner
lives of oak leaves, fern fronds, and canning jars.

There in that crypt-like cellar, at the base
of narrow, rounded stairs fit for a keep,
I was surprised one day to find a darkroom,

and my uncle hard at work, two prints pinned
to a clothesline, fixer and developer
solutions vinegaring the air.

A safe light suspended from a socket;
opaque bottles, plastic trays, bamboo tongs
all laid out beside the utility sink;

and the enlarger, that impromptu beast:
a plywood platform, a heron's neck of pipe,
and a squat head as wide-eyed as an owl's.

What need had we for old film negatives
when a box of photographic paper
could open into story like canvas?

My uncle taught me you didn't need much,
a handful of leaves, perhaps—oak, maple.
Scatter a few on a sheet, then shine your light,

and what seeps into clarity beneath
your gently agitating tongs is not
mere accident or chance but a vision:

the spotlighted ghosts of leaves, not fallen
but falling, floating free perpetually
in the pure black of elemental night.

Or dive into a coffee dark sea
with daisies, mums, and marigolds, once
on fire in that garden on Everett Street,

now a swimming school of luminous
invertebrates. See them cluster? Watch them
wavering at the bottom of a tray.

Or take a pair of chive blossoms, purple
cupola we snip or pinch to foster
new growth. Flash them for thirty seconds,

and they transform into sparklers arrested
the moment before their bonfires of sparks
burst into showers with a crackling hiss.

So many still lifes dripping on newsprint.
Yet so much left to do in the apricot
dimness of that darkroom-for-a-day.

We tried landscapes next—all nocturnes, of course,
the moon as perfect a circle as
the canning jar seal we used to make it.

Call this one *Alpine Crossing*: sprigs of pine,
cedar, and juniper are full-grown trees
staggered on a moonlit slope in summer.

You want to climb those torch-lit crowns
out of the dark of every hill of worry
and shine as they do, brighter than stars.

Call this one *Go*: a sleek greyhound
as bright as the moon or X-rayed bone runs
toward the cellophane snow of a mountain.

So what if it once ornamented the hood
of a 1930s Lincoln? Now it flies
forever in the joyride of a chase.

Call this one *The Long Road Home*: it might be
a moonscape if it weren't for the lake,
the roadside fence, cut-out hills, and paper duck.

See how the stars are as fine as sugar?
The trees have launched like phosphorus missiles.
That curved road carries you straight to the sky.

But my favorite is another still life:
on a table fashioned from brush fringe,
long-stemmed Silver Dollars spill from a bottle—

nothing special and yet so much my uncle
he might as well have signed his name.
Beside the bottle, a pair of duck eggs

where apples or pears might have glistened
in a mood-lit Renaissance painting.
And in the space above, a cigarette

he plucked from behind his ear. He set it
alongside the petals where its shadow
glows diagonally like a U. F. O.

Dried thistle and curling fern, strip of lace
and lavender bloom, oregano and maiden
grass. Cigarette and lighter, clothespin

and rusty nail, coffee mug and empty jar.
Trickle of the stop bath, slick photograph,
pat-pat-pat of drops draining onto newsprint.

The thing itself and what imagination
does to it: my uncle taught me the difference,
and sometimes that difference is all you need.

Egg Tempera

for Jeanne Zychowicz

It smells of worms and straw,
the duck egg she fishes from the chain-linked pen
my uncle built beside her studio.

It is tarnished, too—
not the creamy white of stationary
or salt or store-bought eggs

but the everyday dun
of sand on fine-grained sandpaper,
a thing still close to ground.

She taps it with a spoon
so lightly she coaxes a hairline crack
around the middle,

then splits the shell in two,
each half a cup a small girl might use
to ply her doll with tea.

Next, she passes the yolk
from cup to cup like a jellyfish
jostled at the waterline.

The jagged eggshells
shave off more whites
with each pass

until only the spongy round
remains—orange, slippery, whole,
ready for use.

So it might have been
in *quattrocento* Italy as Old Masters
layered pigments

before the advent
of oils. But we are in Toledo, Ohio,
the old Polish neighborhood,

in the backyard of the house
my great-grandmother gave her granddaughter
because a home should have roots.

Her studio door is open.
The trellis creaks under the weight
of breezes through grape leaves.

Yolk in a halfshell,
she wets the bristles of a medium brush,
bleeds excess water

against the lip of a jar,
and pierces the membrane with the tip.
She will color away

all hints of duck
from this rich base with dabs
of Payne's Grey, Prussian

Blue, Burnt Sienna,
Cadmium Yellow, Sap Green—pigments
for a New England lighthouse

fresh in memory:
tapered white tower, rocky coastline,
storm-tossed rollers

exploding in foam
against crags of tan quartzite,
sea gulls gliding above.

She swirls a circle
of yolk onto the center of her palette,
then trails in a little blue,

a little white, a little grey.
Her colors cream together.
She lifts her brush.

A sky needs
painting. A wave must crash
before our eyes.

Finding Dún Dúchathair

for Anne-Marie Miller-Blaise

Even your ankles would turn medieval on this hike.
No step is certain: scores of limestone slabs
the color of weathered cedar shakes
tilt underfoot like tiles broken loose or
floorboards undermined by decades of neglect.

Your trek sounds like porcelain bobbled.
Any footfall could pitch you sideways as
stone gives way on stone or shoes slip or ram
uneven cobbles over patchy ground.
Fissures here are wide enough to snap bones.

Step by step across flats and gricks you go
with a gingerly, adventurous care,
over low spots in unmortared walls,
across an ancient *chevaux-de-frise*
tumbled like the headstones of the lost.

No one remembers who made the cashel ahead
or against whom it was made. Now it sprawls
across the bleak span like a crocodile
sunning itself between two high-cliffed coves.
You skirt the wall to a field of lush turf.

Around you, sheer cliffs bleed waterfalls.
Herring gulls and kittiwakes cry from nests
and perches on ivory stained ledges.
Some ride the air like untethered kites
above Atlantic as far as you can see.

You have reached the end of this earth, where sea
and sky are two halves of one immensity
marbled in greys and blues. Angling breakers
crash and boom in caverns far below.
Wind is so brisk it fills your eyes with tears.

What word could give you the gift of this place?
I could whisper, *solitude*, but would have
to fur its edges with unceasing eddies
of salt air, grasses as soft as cashmere,
and at least a century of acid rain.

George Herbert on the Church Floor

So, when the others clear the nave,
   he is left alone in swelling
silence. Candlelight flickers against grey
    walls. Watery sunlight through arched
    windows splashes shadows onto
box pews. A lifetime of occasions
    comes down to this: his mouth gone dry,
    his heartbeat sounding in his ears.
In spite of all his preparations,
    all his many nights of prayer
    and pages plied with words he shapes
so well, he stands exposed before the sun
    burst of an altar place, like some
    musician whose lute lacks strings.
What else can he do but prostrate himself
    on the church floor and pray until
    the chill of wood and underearth
seeps through his vestments, and all
    his friends wonder why he lingers.
    The arrow of no sundial,
sand of no hour glass, ticking of no clock
    can plumb the space between his vows
    and where he hopes they will lead.

Lecture Upon a Pigeon

A pigeon lands
on the pier railing near

where weathered fisher
folk rest their rods.

It ratchets looks in all directions,
a shine in its amber eye.

Look closely: even
this pigeon is beautiful.

It hears what we can't,
sees colors deep into ultraviolet,

always manages
to find its way home.

Who among us
can say the same?

With trilled wing-beats,
it flits to a leaking spigot

beside a vacant bench
and drinks the drops

pooling at the mouth.
For a moment

its neck shimmers
purple and green

as vibrantly
as a peacock's tail.

When it flies away,
everything greys again.

Heliotropism

How solid you've become around the trunk,
your whole body thickening like a stalk
to fully support your inquisitive head.
I have to heft you when I walk.
And from my shoulder, your eyes blaze
toward lights, shapes, bits of color or contrast.
Who knows what rays attract your gaze
or how long the sudden sunbursts will last?
Sometimes, little one, what I wouldn't give
to be so enthralled by the ordinary
I would stretch every sinew, break every
grip for a better look. What I wouldn't give
    to penetrate the mire of my adult gloom
      to see what you see, your petal smile in bloom.

Basket

One sweep of the keening weed whacker
cuts down a stand of tall grass,
uncovering the old cradle basket
gone to ground beside the greenhouse.

Handle of thick, braided wicker, sturdy weave
of the lozenge base, it used to have
a blond gloss and an aquamarine blanket
where Pika slept many an afternoon.

You could lift it by this arch,
cat and all, and carry it room to room
or cart it to the car for a road trip,
a piece of home along for the ride.

Now it is driftwood grey, its bowl dense
with campanula stalks. Try to lift it,
and one end of the too-light handle
comes away with the ease of an oiled hinge.

Move it, and it would splinter apart.
Its fraying wicker has loosened its hold
on all but earth, like incense dissolving
in the slow burn of the seasons,

while it waits for the bellflowers to bloom.

Mustard Jug

The gunmetal smell of coinage
    cannot quite
conceal the sweetness of mustard

long gone. This jug, once mustard-rich,
    was emptied
months ago and left for trash. Now

it gutters my grandmother's tips.
    It catches
run-off from her apron pockets

after shifts so tiring she leaves
    her counting
till the electric bill comes due.

I say *jug*, but picture a jar-shaped
    volleyball
with a screw-on, saucer-sized lid.

Picture it old style, ribbed like a
    pumpkin but
dull yellow and heavy as a

cinder block with pennies, nickels,
    and dimes she
collected alongside the crumbs.

Picture my twelve-year-old hands
    heaving it
to the table, its thud against

the laminate top, the dry rasp
    of its threads
as I unscrew the lid. Inside

the level isn't as high as it
    used to be.
The jug once brimmed every month.

Now her take just barely reaches
    two-thirds full.
Yet it will be enough today.

So will the bread she is baking,
    as usual,
from scratch. She breaks eggs into flour

while I upend the jug and sluice
    a crashing
cascade of coins that tumble

and puddle spectacularly
    across half
the table—my favorite part,

perhaps. I prospect the coppery
    moraine for
glints of silver while she sets

aside the first loaves to rise,
    then dumps flour
on the counter to begin again.

She plans to make six loaves today,
    aching feet
from yesterday's shift forgotten.

My uncle says he saw her once
    heft two trays,
fully laden, dish against dish,

on the pedestal of each palm
    all the way
across the crowded restaurant,

weaving in among the tables
    and never
colliding or spilling a spoon.

Today she is ours. Her thick hands,
    dusted white,
work eggs and flour together

until the soft, jiggling dough
    becomes
as smooth as a baby's ass, she says.

And me, me then one more worker
    on her line
but willing to sift, sort, stuff, and

stack coin rolls, lining them neatly
    like stripped logs
my grandmother will mill into

cash—she kneading dough while I poke
    dimes down deep,
my fingers reeking so strongly

this jug, this counting, will flare forth
    whenever
I handle change the rest of my life.

Homemade Wine on the 4th of July

Fireworks downtown above anchored boats
and crowds clotting both sides of the Maumee.
Cracks of gunfire, cannon shots, thudding booms,
pops and blooms of flamed confetti,
ring forts of false daylight drizzling
into darkness above rooftops miles away.

And closer? A world-weary watchfulness.
Ducks murmuring uneasily in their pen,
lone howls of neighborhood dogs sounding
the shoals of city streets. Stray cats and rats
hiding under steps, porches, and hedges,
eyes everywhere yet nowhere to be seen.

Whether it was before or after you
brought out the jug of plum wine you made,
I can't say. But you told tales from books by
Ruth Montgomery, metempsychosis,
the souls of dear ones sky-dancing together
in murmurations lasting whole lifetimes.

And I drank your wine, sweet and syrupy,
like a communion from out of nowhere
yet directly from a shelf in your mudroom,
at home here, at night, where we were shadows
in the shadow of a trellis heaped with vines,
our faces unseen, our talk full of pauses.

Whispers from the trenches of eternity.
Or just stories. The trellis swing creaked.
Pale light flickered on the neighbor's white wall.
The distant crackling built to a frenzy,
then ceased. Silence in the yard. All things end.
Must they? Your cigarette flared one last time.

Speak again of lives passing, and to come.

Stone Trough on Inis Mór

for Sam Green

Hewn for livestock
that graze this field
no longer, it catches
only what rain and wind
provide: a few dead
flies, chickweed heads,
petals of red clover,
and a stray grasshopper
pinwheeling in the murk.
I pluck a stem of grass
gone to seed and offer it
a lifeline. Its every foot
clings to the bristly tip.
It has spent a lifetime
waiting for these seeds,
as though every jump
carried risk of drowning,
as though something
more than luck
had to bring me here,
as though it knew
one grass stem
would be enough
to save us both.

Missing You

Nothing lands right today
or stays in place long enough to matter.
When I crack an egg, half the yolk
falls outside the skillet and burns.
My elbow knocks a cup that lodges
in the drain—I have to free it with pliers.
This seam splits, this zipper breaks,
this toilet clogs, this stack topples,
this cork breaks in the bottle's neck.
Rain falls whenever I step outside.
You are far away from me,
your voice nowhere but in my head,
and my body and my blood
and everything I touch
cannot help but notice.

Birthday Wish

Gusting, whisking, pilfering, the wind
would make a kite of every loose thing.
See how it riffles oaks and maples,
how yellow leaves spring free and firefly,
butterfly in streams across walkways.
You were born during blustery change.
See now how the season celebrates:
the trees offer you their brightest lights
to dazzle your eyes, cushion your feet.

Perfume Bottles

As numerous as raindrops on a window
the sample bottles of fragrances
she used to dab against her veiny wrists
posed like manger scene figurines
on the lace coverlet of her dressing table.

Floral scents perfumed the bedroom
against gathering dust. Atomizers drooped
like overripe figs. Cut glass facets
faded in weakening daylight
like stars yielding to a pre-dawn glow.

Props against a waning dignity.
No one who came later to clear her room
could have treated them with anything like
her care. Nowhere but in my memory
were they safe from being swept away.

Log Ride

for Virginia Lofendo

1

Step down into the fiberglass log still
tethered to the high schooler's levered brake,
and it shimmies like a pony startled
by the heft of you before settling
into the draft of your new partnership.
You lie practically all the way back,
straddling the long, damp vinyl cushion,
your legs wish-boned straight before you,
heels touching the bilge of previous rides.
The lever thrown, and off you go, afloat
on a current coursing a sky-blue trough.

No steering for you. You are thrown flotsam
bound where the water takes you the way
it almost always should into a landscape
larger than yourself. This one is forest.
The motion whispers you to silence.
Motes in dappled sunlight, plash and gurgle,
the log nudges the smooth sides of S curves,
bumps and squeaks along as you sway and glide
without hindrance, no thoughts but green ones,
growing as the trees do: with patience.

And then you slam into a ratcheting lift.

2

They lift the toboggan
        so gently
from the rafters you'd think
        its lacquered
maple would bruise like ripe
        pear skin
if it grazed anything
        other than
my uncles' practiced hands.

All through the drive I fear
        it will fly
off the roof of the van
        and shatter
on the road behind us,
        all traffic stopped.
But now they free it with
        the same care
they used to tie it there.

Afternoon or evening,
        who can tell
this time of year when sleet
        pinpricks cheeks,
and noses and ears go numb,
        and trees
are leafless, black tangles
        against
flat, chai-colored clouds?

Soon the clearing ahead
       disappears
into sky, and strangers
       on shields and
sleds take running starts and
       hurl themselves
over the edge, their shouts
       swallowed like
stones tossed from a bridge.

Our turn. Your brothers load
       my snowsuited
bulk into the hood's crook like
       a warhead.
You slide in behind me,
       your arms firm
around my waist. We hang
       in mid-air,
then plunge, together.

                    3

Hoisted and released, you level again,
float into the mouth of a fiberglass cave
and curve around an animatronic mill:
stutter-spin of the big-toothed rotary saw,
lumberjacks frozen in a dusty pantomime
of milling the same old log to the same
old alpine music. But who cares about them?
You seek the owl-high flight through the trees,
the weightless glide on dry tracks, the plunge
to where all this water feeds.

                    Can you see us now?
Your granddaughter rides in this damp prow,
her hair loose, her grip tight on rusty rails,
arms and shoulders tense in anticipation
of that last, cold, inevitable drenching.
And I shadow her as you shadowed me,
ready to catch, as you did, that last sparrow
of panic with soft encouragement, ready
to share her loud, free, rollercoaster scream.
Here we go—top of the rise. We tilt, then dive
roaring. Our flight gives us thirty-foot wings
of water.

                    They shower us back to earth.

Leaf

Deep along the forest trail
in a spotlight of sunshine,
a yellow leaf, brown-spotted
like a caterpillar's back and
cupped like a Chinese soup spoon,
hangs in mid-air, not quite
fallen. What holds it there
is invisible, much like
what holds up all of us.

Driftwood

Driftwood log like a tusk upthrust
or a whale's jawbone erected
to catch late afternoon sun,

you cast long shadows.
You are a cat's promontory
bolted to a carpeted round,

an island on our Canadian ash floor,
a lost object found by saw and drill,
ratchet and bolt. When we hauled you

from the seaside boneyard,
the Pacific had bleached you
to a hoary blonde. Now you live

in two: your other half presides downstairs.
Your rounded top slowly darkens
from the passage of many hands.

When a cat rakes his claws against you,
they hiss like droplets in an oiled skillet.
Yet the flakes you shed are as soft as cork.

My Aunt, Sketching

She hated making portraits but couldn't resist the cat,
    sprawled and squint-eyed in a grid of sunlight
on the faux marble counter. Air flowing in was feather-light
    against our skin. So was the touch of her pen.
She recalled the old exercise: never lift
    the tip, fashion the whole through one
continuous line. Even on the back of an envelope,
    the only scrap on-hand, she couldn't stop until
all the furrows of personality aligned into whatever
    likeness could be had in blue ballpoint.
Not even the cat's whiskers stymied her. She merely
    backtracked, hardly thickening the line. Then
she wound inward, bunched the line gatherings,
    filled the white space with what looked like fur.
Sure, slow migration of her hand. Steady
    slope of the shaft between thumb and finger. Silky,
faint *scritch* of the point doing its work. Simple
    pleasures of a lazy doodle one long afternoon.
Scents of oregano, rosemary and thyme
    waft in from the garden. I want to hold
this moment, keep my pen moving,
    from margin to margin, down, down
down across thirty years of page toward
    the spider-silk sheen of the tortoise shell face.

What a Hummingbird Knows

for Tony Curtis and Mary Canavan

Not hand sanitizer, or hands,
or the masks we wear
when we venture into stores,
or stores, or muffled breaths,
or the smell of alcohol when we leave

but zip and plunge
from bloom to bloom, sugar
water feeder hung from a rafter,
needlework of beak and tongue,
and the sky-quaking of its heart.

Arts of the Book

Chester Beatty Library, July 2018

Sometime when your hours lack
definition or when rain showers
would keep you inside anyway,

take a stroll past books and scrolls,
armor and ink wells, jade combs
and woodblock prints. In case

after case, leather-bound volumes lie
open like beggars' hands behind glass.
A candlelight of gold leaf warms

their display pages. Learn how
each red is ground azurite,
each green, ground verdigris,

each blue, lapis lazuli. Learn how
the black ink of Chinese calligraphy
came from the soot of fired pine.

Pay attention. Let it steep. Learn
how each page required an artist
and one who can perceive its art.

Awake

Worries gust at 3 a.m.—dry rot
in the wall, bird's nest in the attic,
stacked folders about to fall, no rest
from it all.
                    Hips ache.

                              Eyes sting.

                                        Awake.

But then my winds subside, breaths deepen:

                                        I think of you,
                    though far away,
tossed
          in the whirl of your own busy days.
I see again a circle of sky
shining above my hurricane's eye.

Ice and Stone

The last ice age carried boulders
from the hills of Connemara
across what is now a shallow sea,
over the future graves of fishermen,
past reckonings of grief and longing.

Ice long gone, its hand withdrawn,
they stand like chess pieces
on the limestone squares of Inis Mór,
the game board stalemated
by wind, rain, and time.

In their crimson striations,
in their sunlit flecks of mica,
lies the passion of their first joining;
in their gritty, dusty faces,
the miles traveled, the days since.

So, too, are my thoughts of you,
carried across the sea of our separation.
You can't miss them, glinting
and unbreakable, on the wind-swept,
rain-swept, dream-swept plain of my every day.

Between Two Rivers in Galway

Water gushes from unseen places,
crossing underneath the bank

between Friar's River and the Corrib.
It splatters against tumbled stones.

Wind gusts alder leaves as if
to shake free loose change.

A sea gull kite tethered to a tapered
rod soars above bankside apartments.

It teeters on a table leg of updrafts,
dips and climbs without letting go.

Rain keeps most people
inside this morning.

My sole companions: blustery air
and those who aren't here.

A lone swan on clear water
drifts in to catch what he can.

Rosary

A necklace of cut-glass beads
the pale blue of a lover's eyes
and delicate brass links

pools in my palm with a sound
like rain against fiberglass.
Five decades of *Ave Marias*

she last recited five decades ago
meet on either side of a penny
medallion of the haloed Virgin

within a second oval halo.
From her feet, another chain:
one bead, then three, then one,

then the crucifix, its sinewy
Christ pegged to a cross
ornamented with suggestions

of flowers and ivy leaves.
I drape the rosary across
my outstretched hand

and hold it toward the window.
It feels as light as a handkerchief
and as cool as river stones.

How many hours did
her hands warm these facets
as they eyed the light?

Rainstick of the old faith,
bass rhythm of the five mysteries,
comforter of days in a land

whose language never became her own,
you guided my great grandmother
for years in silence, as one by one

she pinched and rubbed your every
bead between thumb and forefinger
to count without counting

her daily *sotto voce* prayers.

Saturday at Portmarnock

for Mark Pigott

That day clouds the pony grey
of the Irish sea withheld their rain,
but winds gusted fitfully
from all directions, rustling
wild grasses that stood so high
they often hid both sea and estuary.

We hit our balls as best we could
and walked mowed paths between
mounds that glaciers left behind
and Pickeman left untouched
in links laid lightly
across a seaside landscape.

When we reached the fifth tee,
we thought we were lost,
a tee box aimed at a power plant,
no fairway in sight. Screw on
your courage, the guide book said.
Gorse and blackthorn disagreed.

The way forward on or off
any course is just like this:
almost all the tee shots are blind,
so you trust the memory
of ten thousand swings
to land you safely in the short grass.

Sap

Grab hold of this serpent's tail—
it feels like a thing once living.
Its tapered end burns with rust
like a lit cigar inhaling.
Shake it: a rattler's rattle
where the corroding clasp
once linked to a belted chain.
It bends stiffly, seven inches
of braided leather as tight
as muscle and tobacco dark.
No jagged, no sharp edges,
nothing to catch on clothes,
nothing to slow its whiplash
emergence during some wise
guy alleyway brawl.
Set it down—a sharp knock
on wood—its serpent head more
hammer than skull, a plug
of iron wrapped in chapped skin.
I first saw it years ago
when he thwacked the business
end against his palm and said,
One short swipe to the head,
and that bastard goes down.
An heirloom now, it comes
to me, a survivor's tool
a survivor kept long past
his fears, long past his need.

Lines in June

A moment ago this page was blank.
Now I skate across it on the nib
of a fountain pen, sure of direction
(left to right, down one line, across, repeat)
but not of what my lines might dredge
as I pledge myself to words, or they to me.

This line furrows the soft earth of a fast track,
the kind that dries so quickly it lightens
mere minutes after tanker trucks fan water
all along its oval mile. June or July,
those weeks infused with summer haze
when the grandstand on a weekend nearly fills.

And this line rides the diamond-shaped rakes
of three spluttering tractors in staggered
formation as they comb away all traces
of the previous race. Round and round they go
with hypnotic steadiness, their throaty rattles
wafting in with smells of popcorn and cigars.

And this line dots the pleated ground with hoof prints
in the wake of thoroughbreds on post parade:
proud two-year-olds, a chocolate box array
of blacks and browns, their muscles shining.
Jockeys in their multicolored splendor
ride high as the bugler blows his familiar tune.

And this line loads the starting gate. One-by-one
handlers guide horses past the point of no return.
A tense stillness. A held breath. The flag goes up.
The stalls slam open. *Aaaaaaand they're off!*—
exploding into life, a rhythmic blur
of hooves and heads and riding crops snapping.

Soon the field attenuates along the rail,
speeds through the straightaway in two columns,
then the last turn flings the horses wide
like water raveling from a rope. *Anyone's race!*
shouts the caller like a frenzied auctioneer.
They thunder down the stretch, crowd roaring,

clods flying, hooves pounding toward that tight rope
wire stretched above where every race must end.
This line is the photo finish: nine beats
six by a nose. And this, lost wagers tossed
and tumbled like spent aspen leaves. And this
the queue of those trying their luck again.

One line more, a sequel to the rest, trails
behind the gamblers funneling
their reluctant way through the exits
of Arlington Park. This line, the *swish, swish,*
swish of a wide broom sweeping trampled tickets
into piles no one would think of jumping in.

Keepsake

A tuft of fur
in a heart-shaped box—
white, grey strands
on a heart-shaped pillow.
Somehow their softness
recalls my whole hand
buried in her shaggy back
and her long tail thumping.

Somehow I hear
her impatient barks
and heavy panting.
Her ears are arched,
her tongue lolling,
and there at my feet,
her slimy ball, dropped
for the twentieth time.

I snatch it before
she can and wing it far
into the yard. She is all legs
and paws and floppy ears,
unerringly on course, as if
she knows without looking
where it must fly,
where it must land.

Somehow that ball
still soars forty years later
over that patchy ground,
and she is running,
running, running
with all she has
and all she is
to chase it down.

Connemara Village

after Paul Henry

That sunlit village
might be the dream we drive to
at the world's West edge.

Sure, you know the place:
quaint cottages as peaceful
as the flights of geese,

open land all round,
and days as free as grass new
bursting from rich ground.

See it there, past rocks
and shadows, past all the *nos*
you were ever told

and all the woes you
ever stoked with worrying
till each flame seemed new.

You could spend a year
admiring it from afar
and never come near.

So take your time. Don't drive too fast.
Sunshine seldom ever lasts.

Giacometti Love Note

With these letters I can't help myself.
My scrawl storms all spare white space,
coalescing in the two faces
of my moods: one shadowed in doubt,
the other haloed with thoughts of you.
Always your face graces the flaps of
each day I open with trembling hands.
My cigarette burns a seal between
us, stands in for kisses we can't share.

Bereft

His body moves like it always did.
No aftershocks in his hips or knees,
no back spasms, no stiffness of joint,

bearing, or gait. He walks miles sometimes,
eats well enough, manages to laugh.
You wouldn't think he was maimed at all

unless you held his face between your hands,
stared hard into his eyes, and read there
the seismic mutterings of the dark.

Clock

Defunct there on the wall
in an ambient corner,
it has forgotten the sound
of its cuckoos, the heartbeat
of its gears, the cluck and sway
of its light pendulum
struggling to keep time.

Both chains hang in loops
over a wooden maple leaf
on gabled branches like a scarf worn
more for fashion than for warmth.
Both counter-weights—iron pine cones—
are tucked snugly down below
like the legs of a perched hawk.

It gathers dust and silence
in equal measures, an heirloom
stowed safely in plain sight.
Its Roman numeraled face
peers out from leaf and bird
carvings like a Green Man:
3:17, time stopped for fourteen years.

But not for good. Unhook
the long chains, send the pendulum
softly swinging, turn the minute
hand to twelve: a knock and whir,
the little door swings wide,
the little bird chirps
its bell-clear notes as if brand new.

Jackalope

Burly jack rabbit with crowberry eyes
and a full rack of antlers that makes
no sense for burrowing—a lark
for those too gullible to travel
to that wide, flat land of sheet lightning,
dead armadillos dotting the roadside, and
mass migrations of tarantulas at night.

At breakfast she read aloud the postcard
I sent from Texas, meager apology
for a summer spent someplace else. I like
to think he smiled, listening, dressed for work,
second cup of coffee steaming in his hand,
cigarette threading a fine, bluish smoke
through the air above his ash tray.

I like to think his head was full of sunlight
trying to break through the buckeye leaves above
when, minutes later, he opened the driver's side door.
I like to think a song was on his lips
the moment before he bent to climb in. I like
to think my words on that jackalope were not
my last words to him. But they were. He died,

they said, before his head bloodied the asphalt,
before she could cradle him in her arms,
before any sirens could sound
or paramedics could work him over
or neighbors could gather round to watch,
before anyone could whisper,
now you see him, now you don't.

Reading *Ulysses*

for Edwin Weihe

These pages worked free long ago, the press
of your attention too much for a thin crust
of paperback glue. More folder than spine,
the cover encloses loose sheets and quires
in the lamest embrace, cinched tight by two
rubber bands, one pink, one white. Unslip these,
and the book falls open as if on broken
hinges and would avalanche apart
if it weren't properly balanced in both hands.
Whatever episode it opens to,
your unmistakable voice speaks across
many years of practiced meanderings
along the Sandymount margins of Joyce's
polyphonic sea. Not one of these
well-thumbed, dog-eared, lingered over pages
lacks your remarks or underlinings, your
arrows or exclamations in soot-black ink.
Here you mapped sure routes for generations
of students courageous enough to follow you.
And here I am walking beside you too
as once again you highlight the landmarks
and choice encounters of this Dublin
of the mind. You read Bloom's day to pieces,
and now I read the pieces in my turn,
keeping the faith of the shout in the street
and all those mountain flower yeses,
my bar of lemon soap always within reach.

Shelf-Building

for Frank Lofendo

Honeyed in lacquered stain, the pine boards
propped against the apartment wall
looked wet in early morning light
but were dry and smooth to the touch.

You started right in, as always,
balancing the first twelve-footer
across rickety saw horses
and clamping it smartly in place.

Next, to break in my unmarked saw,
you soaped the blade, teeth furrowing
the new white bar of Ivory,
a coarse dust raining from your palm.

The first cut and every cut
that followed you measured twice
and drew your line with the same square
I later relied on for years.

You showed me how keeping faithful
measures meant knowing why the kerf
of the blade matters in choosing
which side of the drawn line to saw.

You showed me how to coax the teeth
as lightly as a skipping stone
across the contrary grain
to start each cut level and true.

You showed me how the span of blade
nearest the grip was the sweet spot,
how it dug in, growling, on each
down-angled thrust, how the steady

hwick-hwack back and forth changed in pitch
as the off-cut began to tilt,
and how to lighten the strokes then
to stop the board from splintering.

One last nick, the new scrap tumbled
cleanly away, clattering on
a pile beside the sawhorse.
The cuts we made were truer than

the walls we built on, remember?
Remember how we had to lift
the topmost two-by-ten over
a drywall hump and settle it

with a mallet to square the corners?
You did a chin-up then to prove
it would hold against an earthquake.
That afternoon, sweating beside you,

I learned how a well-placed screw can
correct a warp, how a clamp can
mimic a hand when you need one,
and how one cut can guide the rest.

And the random lean-to of boards
grew into shelves sturdy enough
to hold all the books I cherish
and all the books I need to write.

www.ingramcontent.com/pod-product-compliance
Lightning Source LLC
Chambersburg PA
CBHW070745030726
47601CB00001B/155